Essential Lives

GLORIA STEINEM

Essential Lives

GLORIA

STEINEM

WOMEN'S LIBERATION LEADER

by Erika Wittekind

Content Consultant:
Amanda Lock Swarr, assistant professor,
Department of Women Studies, University of Washington

ABDO
Publishing Company

CREDITS

Published by ABDO Publishing Company, 8000 West 78th Street,
Edina, Minnesota 55439. Copyright © 2011 by Abdo Consulting
Group, Inc. International copyrights reserved in all countries. No
part of this book may be reproduced in any form without written
permission from the publisher. The Essential Library™ is a
trademark and logo of ABDO Publishing Company.

Printed in the United States of America,
North Mankato, Minnesota
062011
092011

Editor: Mari Kesselring
Copy Editor: Jennifer Joline Anderson
Interior Design and Production: Kazuko Collins
Cover Design: Kazuko Collins

Library of Congress Cataloging-in-Publication Data
Wittekind, Erika, 1980-
   Gloria Steinem : women's liberation leader / by Erika Wittekind.
      p. cm. -- (Essential lives)
   Includes bibliographical references.
   ISBN 978-1-61783-007-5
   1. Steinem, Gloria--Juvenile literature. 2. Feminists--United
States--Biography--Juvenile literature. 3. Steinem, Gloria. I.
Title.

   HQ1413.S675W58 2011
   305.42092--dc22
   [B]
                              2011006297

TABLE OF CONTENTS

Gloria Steinem would become a prominent writer and feminist.

BREAKING FREE

n the mid-1950s, Gloria Steinem's classmates at Smith College in Northampton, Massachusetts, probably could not have guessed where their friend had come from—or where the future feminist was headed. To them,

Steinem seemed a little bit unusual, but bright and personable. She had long, manicured nails, wore heavy eye makeup, and liked costume jewelry while her classmates wore Bermuda shorts, knee socks, and collared shirts. She told funny stories, listened to their problems, and loaned them her clothes. Self-conscious about her background, Steinem tried to blend in at Smith. She hid details about her family. Growing up with such a different set of experiences and coming from a vastly different social class than most of her schoolmates, she felt uncomfortable just being herself. She studied the young women around her for cues on how to act. Her continual pleasantness led one classmate to exclaim, "Why don't you ever get angry? Get angry! Get angry!"[1] It was not until years later that Steinem's classmates would recognize her true potential.

It was somewhat of a miracle that Steinem had landed at an elite women's college in the first place. Steinem had almost no formal education as a young child. Just a year before being accepted at Smith, she had been living in a rat-infested apartment that had no kitchen sink. She had no involved parents making sure she did her homework. Her teenage years were spent taking care of her mentally ill mother. But through hard work and a change in fortune, Steinem had managed to obtain one of the best educations available to a woman in the 1950s.

Fitting In

Steinem was generally happy during her years at Smith College. She enjoyed eating three square meals a day, raiding the library for reading material, and dancing in the dormitories or going to movies with her friends. Because she was so poorly prepared academically, she earned mostly Cs and Ds as a first year student. But she had the natural intelligence to succeed. By her sophomore year, she was on the dean's list. She ended up as one of the top students in her class and would graduate with honors in 1956.

Steinem became quite popular, with several close friends. By senior year, she also had a serious boyfriend. Blair Chotzinoff fell hard for Steinem. He admired her exceptional intelligence so much that at first he feared making a fool of himself. Steinem was smitten, too. Chotzinoff was handsome, funny, and adventurous. A pilot for the Air National Guard, he once rented a small airplane to take Steinem on a date.

The Next Step

Like just about every woman at Smith at the time, Steinem assumed she would someday get married.

Middle- to-upper class white women then, even the educated ones, were expected to marry as soon as possible. Steinem had risen far considering her disadvantaged past. By the standards of the time, she would have been quite fortunate to enter adulthood with a superb education and an adoring husband. So when Chotzinoff proposed, she said yes.

But immediately Steinem felt

Smith College in the 1950s

Smith College was one of the Seven Sisters schools created as female equivalents to the all-male Ivy League universities. Located in Northampton, Massachusetts, Smith College opened its doors in 1875. At the time, the idea of giving women a high-quality university education was groundbreaking. Smith even trained women in fields previously reserved for men, such as math and science. The school had a higher percentage of female professors than most co-ed universities, so students had more role models to look up to.

But these schools were also products of a conservative time. For example, Smith's catalogue in the 1950s proudly proclaimed that there were far more male professors than female, supposed evidence of the quality of education. Graduates were not expected to use their expensive educations to pursue ambitious careers of their own. Most either married right after college, or they left the workforce after just a few years to become wives and mothers, maintaining household roles. The goal of higher education still seemed to be to create ideal women to fill these traditional roles. As Steinem recalled being told while at Smith, "If we're ever to have educated children . . . we must have educated mothers."[2]

uneasy in the role of fiancée. Her friends threw her a bridal shower, and Steinem tried to act the part of the happy bride. Meanwhile, inside, all she felt was dread. It was not her feelings for Chotzinoff standing in the way; the two were clearly in love. But she felt trapped by the very idea of marriage. Years later, she explained to an interviewer:

> *Marriage was the only way a woman could change her life. Therefore once you chose the man you were going to marry, it was the last choice you made. After that you had to follow his work and his friends and his life, and ultimately, your children's lives. And if you really believe that, as we did in the 1950s, it becomes a little death. Because it's the last choice you can make.* [3]

At 22 years old, Steinem hardly knew herself. She was not ready to make that choice. With college ending and no home to call her own, she feared what would come next for her. She felt she had only just started to experience freedom—she could not give it up again so quickly.

Her Own Path

Steinem needed to get away, and she found the perfect opportunity in a fellowship to India.

Steinem was stranded in London in 1956, waiting for her student visa.

Smith was providing $1,000 scholarships to two graduating seniors to study in the Asian country. One of the students had backed out, and Steinem pounced on the opening. She could not stand to face Chotzinoff with her decision, so she left a note and her engagement ring on a table where he would find it. It was the first of many marriage proposals that Steinem would turn down over the years.

Because the scholarship money was not enough to cover airfare and living expenses, Steinem made an arrangement to write publicity materials for an airline in exchange for tickets. The college also had made no plans for what the women would do or where they would live in India. But Steinem trusted that she would figure the rest out when she got there.

On her way to India, Steinem was stranded in London while she waited for her student visa to come through—a document she needed to finish her journey. While she waited, she found a job at a coffee shop to support herself. Weeks passed, and Steinem soon realized that she was pregnant. She was so devastated that she contemplated suicide for the first time in her life. She knew that Chotzinoff would marry her if she told him. But she still did not want to marry him, and she did not want to have a child. After years of caring for her mother, she dreaded the commitment of caring for another human being for nearly two decades.

Alone and in a foreign country, Steinem had a decision to make. It was a decision that would change the course of her life—in more ways than one. Steinem did not know it yet, but she would become a prolific journalist and major advocate for women's rights, including reproductive rights, and various other causes around the world.

Steinem poses with football pennants at a photo shoot in 1965. Steinem's childhood and early adult years were stressful and at times traumatic.

Steinem and her sister, Susanne, left, at Steinem's fiftieth birthday party.

CHILDHOOD

*I*n 1920, Leo Steinem was a student at the University of Toledo, Ohio, where he helped found a campus newspaper called the *Universi-Teaser*. One day, Leo spotted a girl on campus who he thought looked interesting. He found out her name was Ruth Nuneviller and posted a sign on a campus bulletin board asking her to report to the *Universi-Teaser* office. Soon Ruth was the publication's literary editor. Ruth and Leo fell in love and married each other twice—once in front of a justice of the peace immediately after Leo proposed, and again a few months later in front of their families.

Leo worked various odd jobs, while Ruth embarked on a short but successful career at several Toledo newspapers. Ruth used a male pseudonym, because during that time people did not consider women as able to be writers as men. She wrote a gossip column for a tabloid. Then she became society editor at a large daily newspaper and later was hired as Sunday editor. The couple's first daughter, Susanne (Sue), was born in 1925. Ruth continued to work after Sue's birth, but she reluctantly gave up her career when Leo moved the family to Clark Lake, Michigan, to run a lake resort.

Gloria never knew this version of her mother—the bright, ambitious young woman and accomplished journalist. When Sue was a toddler, Ruth had a miscarriage and almost died. Then, in 1929, Ruth witnessed a toboggan accident at the Michigan resort that killed a 17-year-old boy. That same year, her father passed away. Giving up her career and living at the isolated resort might have also contributed to her mental state. Whatever the cause, soon after these events, Ruth suffered a nervous breakdown and started taking tranquilizers. She was never the same again.

LIFE AT THE LAKE

Gloria was born on March 25, 1934, in Toledo. Yet she would spend much of her childhood at the Michigan resort. Life at the resort made for an unusual childhood. Her father had big ideas but was financially irresponsible. Bill collectors called the house and sometimes even came to the door. Leo did not consult Gloria's mother on money matters, and the uncertainty caused great stress to Ruth, worsening her mental condition. Ruth's behavior was unpredictable. At times she was calm enough to attempt housework or to help run the resort. Frequently, however, she was depressed, anxious, or paranoid. The medicine she took affected her speech and coordination. Gloria's parents fought frequently, due to the financial stress and Leo's frustration with Ruth's behavior.

Leo hated cold weather, so each winter when the resort closed the family traveled to California or Florida. Along the way, Leo bought antiques in small towns and sold them for a profit in bigger cities. This arrangement meant that Gloria and Sue never attended a full year of school. They would start each grade in September, and then leave with their parents in November or December. Ruth had a teaching license and claimed to be homeschooling her children, which satisfied officials. When Sue was old enough, she moved into a YWCA to attend a better high school, while Gloria, now the only child at home, escaped into books. From age four, she read anything she could get her hands on. She developed a huge vocabulary, even though she was far behind in basic subjects such as math and geography.

Role Reversal

When Gloria was ten years old, Ruth left Leo, taking Gloria with her. First they moved to Amherst, Massachusetts, to be close to Sue, who had enrolled at Smith College.

Kindred Spirit

As a child, Gloria particularly loved the books of Louisa May Alcott, whom she later called "a kindred spirit."[1] Alcott believed in women's rights and racial tolerance, and she incorporated these messages into her books. Her stories often featured strong, independent women who overcame adversity and were generous toward others. In *Little Women*, the character Jo March at one point announces, "I don't believe I shall ever marry. I'm happy as I am, and love my liberty too well to be in any hurry to give it up for any mortal man."[2] Gloria herself did not marry until she was 66 years old.

Then they spent a summer house-sitting for a friend. When that was over, Ruth took Gloria back to Toledo. They moved into the top level of the dilapidated house that had been Ruth's childhood home. It had been divided into apartments, so Ruth and Gloria lived upstairs and rented out the downstairs. The house was falling apart, with a furnace that had to be condemned by the health department. Rats ran over the beds and in and out of the cupboards.

Ruth's mental health quickly deteriorated. She was often deeply depressed, sometimes hallucinating and unable to function. Leo knew how unwell Ruth was, but he justified leaving his young daughter with Ruth because he did not know how he could earn a living while taking care of either of them. A few relatives lived nearby but rarely offered help, except to buy Gloria some clothes.

When Gloria was 11, she caught a virus and felt ill. She thought her mother might put aside her troubles and take care of her, like a well mother would. But Gloria quickly realized that was not going to happen. "I knew that my mother loved me, but that she couldn't take care of me," Gloria later explained.[3] She would have to take care of both of them.

Making the best of a bad situation, Gloria fashioned some paper curtains for the windows and stacked some books to serve as chairs. She bought cheap food and made her mother simple meals such as bologna sandwiches. The only sink was in the downstairs apartment, so she washed dishes in the bathtub. Despite her efforts, the apartment remained dirty, cluttered, and hazardous.

One summer when Ruth was at her worst, Gloria convinced her to see a doctor. The doctor felt that Ruth should be admitted immediately to a state hospital. But Gloria had read about the horrors of such places, so she took her mother home again. Instead of despairing, she escaped into books and activities. Enrolled at the local school, she worked hard to catch up to the other kids in her grade. She made a few friends and became involved in some school activities, such as the literary society and Girl Scouts. When she was old enough, she worked as a salesgirl. She also earned a little money tap-dancing at nightclubs, a skill she had learned back at the resort.

Planning Her Escape

As a teenager, Gloria dreamed of how she would escape her grim life in Toledo. She earned a little money tap-dancing at local clubs and thought she might make it as a professional dancer. She even tried out for a television show called the *Ted Mack Amateur Hour*, which showcased amateur performers.

FINALLY, AN INTERVENTION

When Gloria was 17, a
neighboring church offered to buy
the house and the land behind it
for $8,000. Ruth wanted to use the
money to send Gloria to college,
but first they had to find another
place to live. Gloria's sister, Sue,
had graduated from Smith and was
working in the jewelry business in
Washington DC. She wanted Gloria
to come live with her and to finish
her senior year at a much better high
school there. Sue tried to convince
Leo to take care of Ruth for a year so
that Gloria could focus on preparing
for college. At first Leo said no;
he and Ruth had been divorced for
years, and he had to work. But when
Gloria started crying—something she
rarely did—he agreed.

Gloria moved in with her sister
and enrolled in Western High
School in Georgetown. There she
relished in her chance to live as a

Friendly Father

Despite Leo Steinem's flaws, Gloria remembers her father with great affection. She wrote in a 1990 essay, "He treated me like a friend, asked my advice, enjoyed my company, and thus let me know that I was loved. Even in the hardest times, of which there were many, I knew with a child's unerring sense of fairness that he was treating me as well as he treated himself."[4] Leo Steinem died in 1962 after being injured in a car accident.

normal teenager. Eager to fit in, she threw herself into schoolwork and activities. Despite being the new student in school, she was popular enough to be voted vice president of the student council and of the senior class. She also joined the French club, archery club, and school yearbook committee. Her years of hardship in Toledo had given her a confidence and maturity that surpassed her peers. Gloria's boyfriend from that time, Ernie Ruffner, described the impression she made:

Family History of Activism

Gloria was not the first supporter of women's rights in her family. Pauline Steinem, her paternal grandmother, was once well known for her support of women's right to vote. Born in Poland, Pauline Perlmutter insisted on attending school over her parents' objections. She married Joseph Steinem, a businessman who had spent time in the United States, and the couple settled in Toledo, Ohio, in 1887. There, Pauline became active in community groups to help the less fortunate and soon took on leadership roles in several organizations. She served on the Toledo Board of Education and campaigned for the inclusion of more women in history books.

Pauline also rose to a leadership position in the Theosophical Society in Toledo. Theosophy mixes a number of religious and supernatural ideas from different cultures. What appealed to Pauline about theosophy is that it emphasized the equality of all people, regardless of gender. This became the basis for Pauline's support of women's suffrage. Pauline once explained, "I believe in woman suffrage because I believe that the perfect equality of men and women is founded on Divine Wisdom. . . . Theosophy teaches first of all the brotherhood of man without the distinction of race, creed, color or sex."[5] Gloria's mother, Ruth, also was a follower of theosophy.

People were in awe of her—she was a thinker and expressed herself well. She was serious but still had a sense of humor. I remember she had strong beliefs and feelings and was very strong-willed.[6]

"Gloria had a social conscience before there was a word for it. She would talk about issues like poverty and race when the rest of us were talking about boys and college. I remember thinking, 'These are such big problems. Why does she even bother to think about them?' She would look at problems and think about how they could be remedied."[7]

—Cyanne Hanson,
classmate at Western
High School

When it came time to apply to college, Gloria's grades were not the best because of the gaps in her education. She had high test scores in English, but lower scores in math, French, and social studies. Stanford and Cornell rejected her applications. But Smith College accepted her, perhaps in part because of her sister's alumna status. In 1952, Ruth moved in with Sue, and Gloria set off to major in political science.

Smith College students take part in a study group in 1948.

When she graduated in 1956, Steinem did not want to fulfill the traditional women's role as caretaker.

INTERNATIONAL
ADVENTURES

After graduating from Smith in 1956, Steinem set out into the world with big plans but few specifics. She had just escaped the role of a traditional wife by breaking her engagement with her fiancé, Blair Chotzinoff, and was on her way to unknown adventures in India. Panic and despair set in when she learned she was pregnant. However, she found out that in England, a woman could obtain an abortion if two different doctors deemed it necessary. She obtained the permissions and had the procedure. It cost her half of her $1,000 fellowship.

After three months in London, Steinem's student visa arrived. When she landed in New Delhi, she had no plans. Since Smith College had not found her a place to live or an academic program, she stayed with people she met along the way. As it turned out, Steinem was happy to have the chance for a broader, more open experience. She ended up seeing much of the country and made many friends. She explained, "The longer I was in India, the more grateful I was for the first advantage of a small, personally administered fellowship such as mine."[1]

Steinem tried to stay away from touristy areas to learn more about what life was like for Indian citizens. As she had done several times in the past, she adjusted herself to her new surroundings. She darkened her hair and wore traditional saris, hoping that it would help her fit in. In one area, she joined a group of activists who, following in the footsteps of the late Mohandas Gandhi, were trying to end caste

Steinem was interested in Gandhi's teachings.

riots. India had a social caste system that deemed
some people inferior to others if they belonged
to certain castes, social classes that they were born
into. When castes fought against each other it would

sometimes result in violent riots. Most followers of Gandhi's teachings did not believe that any group of people should be valued more highly than another group. The group of followers that Steinem met traveled with few possessions, which Steinem found freeing. They held meetings in villages that had been burned during caste riots. As a woman, Steinem was able to go into women's quarters and accompany the women so that they could attend meetings. One woman whose children had been tortured during caste riots told Steinem that she "had never thought anyone outside knew or cared."[2]

Steinem found a few odd jobs in India to pay her way. She wrote essays for the Indian government's travel bureau, modeled in advertisements for Indian products, and found other writing assignments. In 1958, she had earned enough money to pay for her return trip to the United States.

Turning Point

Steinem has considered her trip to India as a turning point in her life. It reinforced her desire to lead an unconventional life and to resist conforming to society's idea of what a woman should be. Her time in India served as the transition from conventional student to radical social reformer. Biographer Carolyn Heilbrun wrote: "Romance, in fairy tales and in most women's lives, assured a 'happily ever after' of marriage that no one was inclined to question or examine closely. If Steinem, however, had a romance, it was with India, with its people, its struggles. . . . India came as close to being Steinem's 'happily ever after' as any other period or event in her life."[3]

High Hopes

Steinem departed India greatly inspired by the social reform efforts she had witnessed there. She realized that it was her calling to be a writer and activist. She was also eager to spread the word about what she had seen in India. However, she was disappointed to find few people interested in hearing about her experiences.

Gloria spent months searching for meaningful work in New York City. She wanted to write, but also to use her experience from India to help make the world

Mohandas Gandhi

Mohandas Gandhi was a leader during the Indian movement to gain independence from Britain in the 1940s. He preached nonviolent forms of resistance such as mass civil disobedience. Gandhi also opposed India's caste system, which gave some people fewer rights than others based on the "caste," or social class, they were born into. Gandhi was assassinated in 1948, becoming a martyr with many followers to continue his work. Even before her trip to India, Steinem was knowledgeable about India's political history from her classes at Smith. She supported Gandhi's nonviolent and democratic methods.

The experiences of her trip made her even more devoted to Gandhi's teachings. Gandhi's nonviolent protest movement influenced her throughout her life, as she supported labor leaders and civil rights activists. It also was a factor in her opposition to the Vietnam War.

Steinem took to heart sayings from the followers of Gandhi, such as "If you do something the people care about, the people will take care of you," "If you want people to listen to you, you have to listen to them," and "If you want people to see you, you have to sit down with them eye-to-eye."[4]

better in some way. She applied for a public relations job with the India Committee of the Asia Society, interviewed with the *Saturday Review*, a popular weekly magazine, and inquired about a series planned by television host Ed Sullivan about countries around the world. No job offers came.

Lacking job prospects in New York, Steinem moved to Cambridge, Massachusetts, to take a job as director of the Independent Research Service in 1959. A nonprofit foundation secretly funded by the Central Intelligence Agency (CIA), the Independent Research Service encouraged US students to attend Communist youth festivals around the world, with the goal of supporting democracy abroad. This was during a time when the Communist-led Soviet Union had a powerful influence, and the United States government was becoming increasingly wary of the spread of communism in other parts of the world. Many worried it could eventually overthrow democracy in countries like the United States. The US students could present a realistic picture of democracy and capitalism in the United States to those who attended the festivals, so that they were not just being exposed to Soviet propaganda.

At first, Steinem had misgivings about the work. Despite the organization's goal, she knew there could be consequences for any US citizen associated with the youth festivals. They could be labeled as Communist sympathizers and be prevented from obtaining government jobs, for example. Considering the anticommunist atmosphere in the United States, she was uneasy about the risk she was taking. But she also considered the work important. Steinem's job included handling media relations and obtaining news coverage of the upcoming International Youth Festival in Vienna, Austria. Part of her job was making sure the public knew that students who participated were not all communists.

On the Scene

The Vienna festival was attended by tens of thousands of young people. In addition to workshops and discussion groups, it featured entertainment ranging from fireworks to opera performances. Biographer Sydney Ladensohn Stern described the atmosphere: "It was a mixture of youthful high spirits, high-minded idealism, Russian thuggery, and hopeless bumbling. A movie version might have been called Mission Impossible Meets Animal

House or Campus Commie-Fighters Con Communists."[5] The grounds were crawling with Soviet spies monitoring the activities. The Communist countries used creative and sometimes forceful methods to keep their delegates separate from other attendees. They also threw parties to lure US students away from important meetings they were holding. Guards questioned the delegates' credentials and controlled what kinds of photographs were taken.

In Vienna, Steinem ran the International News Bureau outside of the festival, issuing press releases and helping media personnel. The Soviets did not allow journalists inside the festival, so she helped reporters set up interviews with delegates. She also assisted the Austrian newspapers in countering the festival's official newspaper, which was preprinted by the Soviets. The operation was

Disappointment in New York City

Steinem was drawn to New York City because of its supposed diversity and wealth of opportunities. But even New York had few opportunities for ambitious young women with radical ideas in the late 1950s. The feminist movement had not yet taken root, and the civil rights movement had barely begun. Most middle- and upper-class white women, like Steinem, married and moved to the suburbs, while jobs that required a college education were reserved primarily for men. Poor women and women of color usually worked, but only in low-status service jobs such as housekeeping or waitressing.

considered a success. The bureau's efforts not only made sure that democratic ideas were represented, but they also provoked the Communists into showing their restrictive and forceful natures. It was a success for Steinem, as well. She gained a reputation for being resourceful and talented under great pressure. She also made some important connections that would help her career as a journalist. ⌐

Steinem's work for the Independent Research Service
was secretly funded by the CIA.

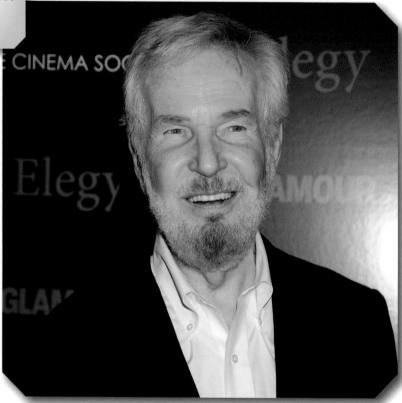

*Steinem started dating Robert Benton in the 1960s.
Benton would become a screenwriter and director.*

AN ASPIRING WRITER

In 1960, Steinem returned to New York
City with renewed determination to
make it as a writer. Through a mutual friend, she
met *Esquire* editor Harold Hayes and his wife Susan.
The couple introduced Steinem to others in the

magazine business, including Harvey Kurtzman, the cartoonist who created *Mad* magazine. Kurtzman hired Steinem to write captions and arrange photo shoots for a new magazine called *Help!* She also wrote some small assignments for *Esquire*, such as captions for fashion spreads and recipes for bachelors, but they were not the kind of pieces she wanted to write.

During this time, she started dating Robert Benton, *Esquire*'s assistant art director. Steinem felt she had a lot in common with Benton, more than she'd had with Blair Chotzinoff. Benton supported her writing and encouraged her to just be herself and stop hiding her troubled past. The supportive relationship worked both ways—Benton credits Steinem as the first person who encouraged him as a writer. He went on to write and direct movies, including Oscar winners *Bonnie and Clyde* and *Kramer vs. Kramer*. The pair worked together on several humorous pieces for *Esquire* and *Show*. One of their articles, "The Student Prince, or How to Seize Power Through an Undergraduate," advised college students on how to fake an interesting personality.

In 1962, Benton and Steinem started talking about marriage. But the idea did not appeal to Steinem then any more than it had when she graduated from college. Thirty years later, Steinem reflected on her reluctance:

Betty Friedan

While Steinem was starting her writing career in New York, another Smith graduate was actively influencing the US feminist movement. Betty Friedan published her book *The Feminine Mystique* in 1963. In this book, Friedan details the societal expectations that confined many women to the roles of wives, mothers, and homemakers, and limited their career options outside the home. A *New York Times* obituary upon Friedan's death in 2006 summarized:

> The portrait she painted was chilling. For a typical woman of the 1950s, even a college-educated one, life centered almost exclusively on chores and children. She cooked and baked and bandaged and chauffeured and laundered and sewed. She did the mopping and the marketing and took her husband's gray flannel suit to the cleaners. She was happy to keep his dinner warm till he came wearily home from downtown. The life she led, if educators, psychologists and the mass media were to be believed, was the fulfillment of every woman's most ardent dream. Yet she was unaccountably tired, impatient with the children, craving something that neither marital sex nor extramarital affairs could satisfy.[2]

Then, you couldn't really remain yourself in a free way, as you can now. It's not easy now, but it's possible. It wasn't just compromising—I can deal with compromising. It was giving up your entire professional life, your name, your identity. It wasn't just compromises. It was surrender.[1]

BUDDING CAREER

In 1962, Steinem published her first major writing assignment in *Esquire*. Called

"The Moral Disarmament of Betty Coed," it was about birth control and sexual behavior on college campuses. Features editor Clay Felker thought she would be ideal for the assignment because she had attended Smith, an all-women's school. Steinem did not yet identify herself as a feminist at that time, but her article contained some of her early feminist ideas about how women could take control of their bodies and reproductive choices through new contraceptive methods.

In the meantime, the Independent Research Service was gearing up for the next youth festival in Helsinki, Finland. Steinem volunteered to help in her spare time and to work at the festival itself. She recruited college students, including future managing editor of the *Washington Post* Robert Kaiser, to write for the festival newspapers. She also talked Felker into helping out, and he ended up being greatly impressed by

Almost Famous

Steinem wanted to be known for her writing, but she also gained attention for her beauty and style and for the prominent men she dated. As early as 1960, a syndicated news article was head-lined "Pretty Girl Genius Helps Edit *Help!* for Tired Minds." It described 26-year-old Steinem as a "willowy beauty . . . [who] is a national magazine editor and a specialist in international politics."[3] In 1964, *Glamour* ran an article about her called "New York's Newest Young Wit." But the piece focused more on her clothing and makeup than on her intelligence.

Steinem's work in Helsinki. "Gloria has incredible political savvy and a seemingly effortless ability to organize and get people to do what she wants them to do," Felker has said.[4] Felker's admiration led him to hire her as a political reporter for his new publication *New York* magazine years later.

Steinem started to receive more assignments, although she struggled to be taken seriously. She wrote a few political pieces, such as an account of the Helsinki festival. But most editors assigned her topics traditionally thought of as interesting to women, such as celebrities, fashion, and homemaking. Her work frequently appeared in *Glamour* magazine, which made her a contributing editor. She enjoyed writing humorous advice pieces about life as a single girl, such as "How to Put Up With/Put Down a Difficult Man."

Going Undercover

In 1963, Steinem got her biggest assignment yet, for which she is still well known today. The editorial board at *Show* was trying to decide how to cover the opening of a new Playboy Club in New York. The Playboy Club was a restaurant and bar where the waitresses, called Playboy Bunnies, dressed

For her first big writing assignment, Steinem went undercover as a Playboy Bunny at one of the popular clubs owned by Hugh Hefner, center.

in revealing bunny costumes. Steinem jokingly suggested they hire journalist Lillian Ross to go undercover and report on the club's inner workings. The editors loved the idea—but they had someone else in mind to pose as a Playboy Bunny.

Steinem agreed to the assignment and applied for a job as a Playboy Bunny, using a false name and lying about her age. To her surprise, she got the job. She spent the next month living the less-than-glamorous life of a Bunny and asking as many questions as she could without arousing suspicion. Her two-part exposé detailed everything from the harsh demerit system through which the women were penalized for not following rules, to the costumes that were so tight that they cut off circulation to the legs. Her articles also described the demeaning way the Bunnies were treated. In one incident, Steinem descended a staircase near a window that made her visible from the street below. A supervisor said, "Go back up and come down again. . . . Give the boys a treat."[5] To disobey would have gotten Steinem in trouble with her supervisor.

The Bunny Experience

After Steinem wrote about life as a Playboy Bunny, exposing the sexist and demeaning treatment of women at the club, she was surprised to receive letters from women asking how they could obtain jobs as Bunnies themselves. Steinem wrote one woman a discouraging letter: "At best, you are a glorified waitress, and at worst a sort of Pop geisha who is encouraged to go out with anybody who could do the club any good."[6]

Afterward, Steinem regretted taking the assignment. It brought her a lot of attention and was even made into a movie, *A Bunny's Tale*, in 1985. But Steinem complained that she had trouble getting serious assignments after her articles on the Playboy Club came out. The media began referring to her as a former Playboy Bunny, not recognizing that she took the gig as a journalist. *Show* had planned to have Steinem write an exposé on the US Information Agency and its conservative leanings, but instead started giving her lighter topics. At a time when widespread sexism made it difficult for women to become successful journalists, Steinem feared that the Playboy exposé had hindered her even more. When an interviewer pointed out, "That piece put you on the map." Steinem replied, "Well, it was the wrong map."[7]

Despite this, Steinem continued to get assignments from *Glamour*,

Landmark Legislation

In 1960, women earned 59¢ for every dollar men made. The Equal Pay Act was signed into law in 1963 as an attempt to end this wage disparity between men and women. The following year, Title VII of the Civil Rights Act of 1964 outlawed employment discrimination based on race, creed, national origin, or gender. Ironically, the reference to gender had been added by a Congressman who opposed the law. He had hoped that the bill would not be passed if it included a prohibition on sex discrimination. However, it did become law, and the Equal Employment Opportunity Commission was created to enforce it. While one-third of the complaints received by the commission came from women, the commission focused primarily on addressing racial discrimination.

as well as from the *New York Times* magazine and *Ladies' Home Journal*. She wrote about pop culture and profiled celebrities including Barbra Streisand, Truman Capote, and James Baldwin. But she also wrote pieces that she found embarrassingly frivolous, such as a 1964 article about textured women's stockings. Fortunately, Steinem's career was only just beginning.

Steinem's writing career began in the early 1960s.

Mourners of Martin Luther King Jr.'s death march near Harlem
in 1968. Steinem reported on the public's response to the tragedy.

POLITICAL ACTIVISM

Steinem's journalism career so far had
turned out to be more of a way to pay
the bills than to promote her ideals. But she
continued to be active on the issues that mattered
to her.

Steinem joined the growing movement to protest the United States' military involvement in the Vietnam War. In 1967, Steinem participated in an antiwar demonstration in Washington DC called Women's Strike for Peace. She also encouraged other writers and editors to pay only part of their taxes as a symbolic refusal to fund the war. More than 400 decided to join the protest.

One of Steinem's other passions was the civil rights movement. When Martin Luther King Jr. was assassinated in 1968, she went to the predominantly African-American neighborhood of Harlem in New York City to report on the fallout.

In 1968, Clay Felker founded *New York* magazine and asked Steinem to work for him. Felker had been in Helsinki with Steinem in 1962, and he admired her work. He was one of the first men to truly see and treat her as a professional equal, recognizing her writing talent as well as her political instincts. In addition to assigning her feature stories, he decided to make her a political columnist for *New York*. Finally, Steinem had the opportunity to cover the subjects about which she cared most. She could report on issues affecting women and other disadvantaged groups.

The Women's Strike for Peace in 1967 was an attempt to get government officials to end US involvement in the Vietnam War.

Presidential Politics

In 1968, Steinem attended the Democratic National Convention in Chicago, Illinois, where the Democrats would select a candidate for the presidential election. Front-running candidate Robert Kennedy had been assassinated three months before the convention, leaving George McGovern, Eugene McCarthy, and Vice President Hubert Humphrey as the top contenders. Steinem was at the convention to support George McGovern, an antiwar politician whom she had helped with fund-raising and speechwriting. She and other McGovern supporters thought rival Democratic candidate Eugene McCarthy seemed insincere in his opposition to the war. The McGovern campaign used one of Steinem's quotes on campaign buttons that read, "McGovern: He's the REAL McCarthy."[1] But Vice President Hubert Humphrey ended up winning the Democratic nomination for president.

Romances

During the 1960s, Steinem had relationships with several talented and prominent men. These included Viking Press owner Tom Guinzberg, *Saturday Night Live* writer Herb Sargent, presidential speechwriter Ted Sorensen, and Broadway director Mike Nichols. In 1968, she had a relationship with activist and Olympic gold medalist Rafer Johnson, whom she met at the Democratic Convention.

After McGovern's presidential chances ended, Steinem worked for his Senate campaign in South Dakota. When he ran for president a second time in 1972, McGovern invited her to join his campaign again. But one of his advisers, Abraham Ribicoff, nixed the idea, declaring, "No broads."[2] Unfortunately, Ribicoff's comment was typical of the sexism in politics of the time. Steinem later remarked, "McGovern accepted it—though he never would have accepted 'No blacks' or 'No Jews.'"[3]

In the fall of 1968, Steinem covered Republican candidate Richard Nixon for *New York* magazine. She tried to get a one-on-one interview with him, as was usually given to the reporters who traveled with him. Instead, she was offered an interview with his wife, Pat. While not the article she had hoped to write, her profile of Pat Nixon became famous because of Pat's honesty about her difficult early life.

HELPING CESAR CHAVEZ

Also in 1968, Steinem became involved in a movement led by Mexican-American activist Cesar Chavez to improve the lives of migrant

---

Violence at the Convention

The 1968 Democratic National Convention in Chicago came at a time of extreme unrest. Martin Luther King Jr. had been assassinated in April, igniting riots across the country. Presidential candidate and civil rights advocate Robert Kennedy had been assassinated in June. Anger about the Vietnam War was at a fever pitch.

In August, approximately 10,000 antiwar demonstrators converged on Chicago during the convention, and 23,000 police officers and National Guard members were there to maintain order. Rioting broke out between the demonstrators and police. Police tried to control the situation with tear gas and mace, but violence erupted on both sides. Even journalists such as Mike Wallace and Dan Rather were roughed up by police during the skirmishes.

While passing out literature on behalf of farm laborers, Steinem was shoved by security guards and ended up with her glasses broken. But she watched most of the violence from a hotel window. From there she could see bystanders being shoved through glass windows below.

farm laborers. Farm workers labored long hours for less than minimum wage and lived in run-down shacks provided by their employers. They had no medical care, and many suffered adverse effects from pesticides. The laborers, many of whom were illegal immigrants with no formal education and little or no fluency in English, were powerless to change their situation.

Chavez, who had grown up in a family of migrant farm workers, was now campaigning for the workers' rights and helping them unionize. Like Steinem, Chavez believed in Gandhi's nonviolent forms of protest. To support a group of grape pickers who were going on strike, he organized a widespread boycott of table grapes. Steinem took an interest after meeting Marion Moses, a fund-raiser whom Chavez had sent to New York to promote the boycott. Moses had struggled to raise money since arriving in New York and even had trouble covering her meager living expenses. One contact suggested

High Profile

In 1965, *Newsweek* published a full-page profile of Steinem—an unusual level of coverage for a young freelance writer. Titled "News Girl," the article painted a glowing picture: "Gloria Steinem, a striking brunette of 30, is as much a celebrity as a reporter and often generates news in her own right. . . . Miss Steinem is a magazine writer and her subjects often become vociferous fans. 'She's the smartest, funniest, and most serious person I know,' says [Mike] Nichols, 'and she looks great.' . . . Says Julie Andrews, 'I think I'd like to be her if I weren't me.'"[4]

she call Steinem, who returned her call right away and offered help.

Steinem picketed outside grocery stores and used her media contacts to help provide publicity for the grape boycott. Because of her efforts, *Time, Life,* and *Look* all did stories, and Chavez appeared on the *Today Show*. The publicity helped spread the boycott, and being in the public eye helped protect farmworkers against any threat of violence by the growers they worked for. Steinem helped Moses organize a benefit that raised more than $30,000. She even let Moses stay at her apartment for four months.

In May of 1969, Steinem went to California to help publicize a march organized by Chavez from the city of Delano to the Mexican border. Steinem slept on oily garage floors until reaching a motel where she could set up a small press operation and work the phone, calling reporters and celebrities. Chavez wrote a personal letter thanking Steinem for her help. Steinem offered additional help with rallies and benefits over the next several decades. ⌒

By 1970, Steinem had a firm background in activism.

Steinem became involved in the women's liberation movement.

FINDING FEMINISM

While Steinem's activities in the
1960s were not all directly related
to women's rights, they laid the foundation for her
involvement in the feminist movement. While she
supported Chavez's cause, she disagreed with his

conservative views on women and his opposition to contraception and abortion. She was disillusioned by the way women were sidelined at the 1968 political convention. And she had spent years fighting to be taken seriously as a journalist instead of being confined to writing about frivolous topics deemed appropriate for women.

But it was not until the end of the decade that Steinem found her calling and her voice as a feminist. In 1969, a radical group called the Redstockings tried to be heard at a New York legislative hearing on abortion. When only one woman—a nun—was allowed to testify, they decided to conduct their own hearing. Steinem attended the resulting speak-out to write about it for her political column. The topic struck a chord with her because of her own experience obtaining an abortion in London. In her later book *Outrageous Acts and Everyday Rebellions*, she describes the experience:

"Women who write, like Negroes who write, are supposed to be specialists on themselves, and little else. Newspapers and magazines are generous with assignments on fashion, beauty and childbirth. (Would men like to write about hunting, shaving, and paternity?) But scientific or economic or political stories have a way of gravitating somewhere else."[1]

—*Gloria Steinem, 1968*

I sat in a church basement listening to women stand before an audience and talk about desperately trying to find someone who would help them [since obtaining an abortion was illegal], enduring pre-abortion rapes from doctors, being asked to accept sterilization as the price of an abortion, and endangering their lives in an illegal, unsafe medical underground. . . . If one in three or four adult women shares this experience, why should each of us be made to feel criminal and alone? How much power would we ever have if we had no power over the fate of our own bodies?[2]

Spreading the Word

It was a powerful turning point for Steinem, who immediately threw herself behind the women's liberation movement. Steinem learned everything she could about the movement by reading feminist writings and by talking to as many feminists as she could find. All her life she had been making her own choices and forging her own path; now she started standing up for other women's rights to exercise power over their own lives. She began writing and speaking in support of a number of women's issues, including meaningful work opportunities for women, equal treatment in the workplace, reproductive freedoms, and protection from violence and harassment.

In 1969, she wrote a news article titled "After Black Power, Women's Liberation" for *New York* magazine. The article won a Penney-Missouri Journalism Award for being one of the first mainstream reports on the growing women's movement. Some of her male colleagues were less supportive, encouraging her to stop covering radicals and get back to serious journalism. But their reaction only

National Organization for Women

In 1966, prominent women gathered for the third annual Conference on the Status of Women. Attendees were unhappy with the government's failure to enforce the prohibition against gender discrimination passed by Congress two years prior. They wanted to create a national organization that would lobby for women's rights. Led by Betty Friedan, several of these women founded the National Organization for Women (NOW).

NOW was made up of mostly middle- to upper-class white women who were housewives or professionals. Their initial goals included encouraging women's participation in politics, ensuring equal opportunities for education and employment, and standing up for the legal rights of women. NOW's mission was more moderate than that of the younger, more radical feminist groups created at the time. NOW members were liberal feminists. That meant they wanted to work within existing social and political frameworks. Radical feminists, on the other hand, believed that change could only occur by completely abolishing these frameworks. They believed that because society was so rooted in the patriarchal system, simply electing more women to political office or getting equal wages as men could not change women's oppression. Everything would need to change.

fueled her determination, as she recognized all the slights she had endured over the years as a woman: lower pay, landlords who would not rent to her, assumptions based on her looks, pressure to marry and settle down, sexist jokes. The list went on.

In 1970, her published pieces included "Why We Need a Woman President," in which she wrote, "Surely a woman in the White House is not an impossible feminist cause. It's only a small step in the feminist revolution."[3] That year, *Time* magazine printed her article, "What It Would Be Like if Women Win." Later, she learned *Time* had paid her less than it paid male freelancers.

Other publications were not receptive to this new direction in Steinem's work. Their responses included, "Sorry, we published our feminist article last year," or "If we

Personal Persuasion

In addition to writing and speaking, Steinem often used her persuasive abilities on a very personal level. When she and friend Dorothy Pitman Hughes met a social worker who admitted he did not want his fiancée to work after they were married, the pair went to work convincing him otherwise. Later, Steinem received a note from the man's fiancée, saying, "Thank you, now I can marry him."[4]

publish one article saying women are equal, we'll
have to be objective by publishing one right next
to it saying they're not."[5] Not to be discouraged,
Steinem started spreading the word through
speaking engagements. She was terrified of public
speaking, so she invited fellow activist Dorothy
Pitman Hughes to speak with her. Hughes had
opened a childcare center for working mothers.
Since Hughes was African American and Steinem
was white, their partnership could demonstrate
that the women's movement applied to all women,
regardless of race.

After their first speaking engagement at New York
University, Hughes and Steinem received invitations
to talk at numerous other college campuses. The
events turned into two-way conversations, as
audience members asked questions and shared their
own stories. Women described instances of date
rape, sexual harassment, and domestic violence—
although none of these terms were in use at the
time. "They were just called 'life,'" Steinem later
noted.[6] Many speaking events were accompanied
by luncheons, press conferences, and cocktail party
fundraisers. Afterward, Steinem often stayed up late
talking to women they had met.

Steinem went on tour with Florynce Kennedy.

When Hughes left to spend time with her children, Steinem went on tour with a series of other speaking partners. These included author and lawyer-turned-activist Florynce Kennedy and civil-rights activist Margaret Sloan, who had just come out as a lesbian.

Face of the Women's Movement

Not entirely by choice, Steinem quickly became one of the most visible leaders of the women's movement. She played a key role in influencing media coverage, raising money, and drawing attendance. Her beauty and charismatic personality helped the movement reach the mainstream public. Her very existence showed people that feminists were not just bitter women who could not find husbands, as many adversaries claimed. As a successful professional herself, she also had become a role model. When she testified before the US Senate at the Equal Rights Amendment hearings in 1970, she became even more visible. Members of the national media were looking for a face to put to the story, and hers was often the one they chose. Numerous magazines ran long profiles of her, and *McCall's* made her its 1972 Woman of the Year.

Her fame brought with it character attacks. She was accused of being too ambitious, a social climber who only dated men who could help her career.

Celebrating Women's Suffrage

August 26, 1970 was the fiftieth anniversary of the ratification of the women's suffrage amendment. Friedan, president of NOW, decided to mark it by organizing a one-day nationwide strike. She wanted women everywhere to walk away from the responsibilities of their jobs and homes for one day to show the invisible importance of women's daily work. In the evening, thousands of women marched in New York City. Steinem was a speaker at the event.

Even Betty Friedan, who had fueled the women's movement with her best-selling book *The Feminine Mystique*, was lukewarm toward feminism's new spokesperson. "Gloria has not advanced any new ideas in the women's movement—but she's an outstanding publicist," Friedan said.[7]

Beginning in the 1970s, Steinem made many public appearances to discuss her causes.

Steinem and Pat Carbine, right, worked together on Ms. magazine.

A New Kind of
Women's Magazine

fter every speaking engagement,
Steinem returned with handfuls of
slips of paper—contact information for women she
intended to help. Letters and phone calls poured
in from others. Some needed referrals to lawyers or

social workers for problems such as abuse, rape, and divorce; others sought information on how to set up nonsexist childcare or resources to combat domestic violence. In 1970, Steinem and her friend Brenda Feigen hatched an idea to reach more women with this sort of useful information. The Women's Action Alliance was born.

Steinem and Feigen considered starting a newsletter to raise money to support this new group. A newsletter would have been easy to publish and a straightforward way to distribute information. But Feigen thought they could do better. She envisioned a glossy magazine featuring in-depth coverage, exploring different viewpoints, and providing a valuable forum for women. Another colleague of Steinem's, *McCall's* editor Pat Carbine, was also pushing the idea. Steinem had not set out to start a magazine. Comfortable as a freelancer, she was wary of committing to a project so large. But the idea of a new kind of women's magazine was appealing. She met with editors, writers, and activists at her apartment and discovered that she was not the only one frustrated with writing for male-run publications. Overwhelmed by their enthusiasm, she began plans for the magazine that would be called *Ms.*

Steinem, Carbine, and public relations executive Betty Harris became the founding partners, but they had difficulty financing their idea. Most businessmen did not think there was a market for a feminist magazine and were wary of a business venture run entirely by women. But *New York* magazine editor Clay Felker came through with a solution. *New York* always published a double issue in December, and Felker offered to publish a sample issue of *Ms.* inside of this issue. *Ms.* would also be sold at newsstands under its own cover, and

Naming the Magazine

The founders of *Ms.* considered a number of names for their new magazine. These included *Everywoman*, *Sisters*, *Lilith*, and *Sojourner*. But Steinem pushed to name the magazine *Ms.* The term "Ms." had been around for several decades to refer to a woman without indicating her marital status, but it was not widely used at the time. In the magazine's early days, *Ms.* employees often found themselves explaining the title's meaning—and that it was not a shortened form of the word "manuscript" or an abbreviation for a medical condition. They even had to tell people how to pronounce it. Author Mary Thom, an editor at *Ms.* for many years, wrote about the symbolic significance of the name:

> *Ms.* clearly broke with tradition, fairly screaming that this was more than just another women's magazine. The *Ms.* woman was independent. She would not be defined by her relationship, or lack of it, to a man, be it husband or father. . . . The statement was a bold one at a time when, for example, women routinely were denied credit in their own names. Merely explaining what the name meant became an opportunity to change minds.[1]

the two magazines would split any profit before parting ways.

The First Issue

Steinem and her partners went to work crowding the preview issue with content, knowing it might be both their first and last shot. In one of its attention-getting efforts, that first issue included a two-page spread titled "We Have Had Abortions," in which 53 women admitted ending their pregnancies illegally. In addition to Steinem, the names included singer Judy Collins, tennis player Billie Jean King, and several famous authors. Steinem, who had kept her abortion secret all these years, warned her mother and sister before the article came out.

Other articles covered feminist issues regarding marriage and children, discrimination at work, and political issues ranging from welfare to war. Jane O'Reilly wrote the popular article "The Housewife's Moment of Truth," in which she described the

Cover Art

Steinem won a disagreement with Felker over the cover art for the preview issue. The initial cover design showed an anxious couple with their backs to each other, with a thick rope binding them together. The headline read: "Breaking the Ties that Bind: Write Your Own Marriage Contract," and Felker wanted the article to be the lead story. Steinem thought the article was not radical enough, so it and the picture ended up inside the issue. Instead the lead story was "Jane O'Reilly on the Housewife's Moment of Truth." The cover art, a painting by Miriam Wosk, showed a weeping, blue-skinned woman with eight arms performing a number of housewife's tasks.

mundane moments that turn housewives into feminists. Another article, "How to Write Your Own Marriage Contract," showed women how to work out issues of housework, finances, and children before the wedding.

The cover was dated simply "Spring 1972" since no one was sure how many months it would sit on newsstands. As it turned out, they need not have worried. On a trip to promote the magazine in San Francisco, Steinem was shocked that she could not find copies of the magazine anywhere. She frantically called Felker, who found out that the magazine had already sold out. It took a mere eight days for all 300,000 copies to disappear from newsstands nationwide. More than 25,000 readers returned subscription cards and checks. The magazine also received more than 20,000 letters from readers. To put that in perspective, *McCall's* had a circulation of 7 million and typically received a few hundred letters per issue.

Challenges of a Startup

After much deliberation, Carbine decided to leave her cushy job at *McCall's* to be editor in chief of *Ms.* She and Steinem bought out Harris after some personality conflicts and went looking for financial backers. Some companies offered millions of dollars for the magazine—but only if Steinem and Carbine gave up control. Finally, they accepted an offer that gave Warner Communications 25 percent interest in *Ms.* for $1 million. The staff began frantic preparations for the first stand-alone issue of *Ms.* to come out in July.

In these early days, the *Ms.* staff had very little structure. Its founders believed in equality, so everyone was an editor and no one was a secretary. Some of the staff had writing and editing experience, but many were just passionate about the cause. Before the magazine started having a regular payroll, it was possible to just show up, start working, and become part of the staff by default. Rita Waterman, who joined the *Ms.* staff after working at *McCall's*, described one of the early meetings:

> *Amid cartons, piles of paper, and general debris, about a dozen women sat on desks,*

Nancy Reagan's Reaction

Fellow Smith College alumna and future First Lady Nancy Reagan gave an interview to a California newspaper after the *Ms.* preview issue. Her husband was then the governor of California. Reagan said she supported equal pay and employment opportunities for women but otherwise disagreed with feminists. "After that, they lose me. I think they are a lot of terribly unhappy women making terribly unhappy men and children. I think it is very dangerous as far as the country is concerned."[2] Reagan represented the views of a significant constituency of conservative women.

a few chairs, . . . and the floor. Most were young (twenty-ish), and . . . didn't know fudge about getting out a magazine. But BOY! Do they have article ideas![3]

Unfortunately, editorial content was the least of their worries. Without the resources of *New York*, they had to arrange their own production, advertising, printing, and subscription services. With no advertising representatives on staff yet, Steinem and Carbine made the sales calls. They faced an unusual challenge. Advertisers were used to paying a rate of approximately two dollars for every 1,000 subscribers at traditional women's magazines such as *Ladies' Home Journal* or *Good Housekeeping*. Meanwhile, magazines such as *Esquire* charged more than $11 per 1,000 readers. Steinem and Carbine felt *Ms.* deserved to make that much money, as well. They had to convince advertisers that reaching *Ms.*'s female readers was worth the extra expenditure. Reaching out to advertisers who wanted to target an educated, higher-income audience, they landed ads from Coppertone, Panasonic, AT&T, and several liquor and cigarette companies. Finally, the *Ms.* editors would be paid.

Steinem worked hard on her vision for Ms.

Steinem was cofounder of the National Women's Political Caucus.

An Embattled Leader

In the beginning, Steinem—who simply loved the freedom of freelancing—vowed that she would spend no more than two years with *Ms*. But she also had trouble refusing anyone who needed her help. And the fledgling magazine desperately needed her contacts and name recognition to succeed. In addition to her other roles, Steinem quickly became the magazine's spokesperson. Anytime she was traveling, whether it was to deliver a lecture or to support a political candidate, she would take time to promote *Ms.* On top of that, because of her fame, many advertisers requested personal meetings with her. Often she ended up traveling far and wide on sales calls, only to find out she was merely satisfying the curiosity of someone who had no intention of buying ad space.

In addition to supporting the magazine, Steinem continued to be very involved in the National Women's Political Caucus, which she cofounded, and in the Women's Action Alliance. She also spent time lobbying for the Equal Rights Amendment (ERA), which would have guaranteed equal rights and protection under the law regardless

Hiring Practices

In its early days, a young man applied for a number of positions at *Ms.* in an effort to reveal discrimination against men in the magazine's hiring practices. Fearful of a lawsuit, Steinem created a gender-neutral list of job qualifications. Some referred to publishing experience, and flexibility on pay and working conditions. Others included a "belief that women of all racial groups are full human beings," "experience and/or knowledge of the cultural, economic and political consequences of growing up female in a sexist society," and "enthusiasm for the magazine's potential in helping women to develop themselves as individuals, and improve the quality of life around them."[1] The editors agreed that men who met these qualifications deserved to be hired. Over the years, men have worked in the business office and in the art department, as well as occasionally as writers and illustrators.

of gender. The amendment was approved by Congress in 1972, but still needed to be ratified by 38 states to become part of the Constitution. As of 2010, the ERA has never been ratified.

Mary Peacock, who worked at *Ms.*, described how overworked Steinem was during this period:

> *Gloria was a combination of working journalist and champion of ideas. The poor woman had so much to do, so many responsibilities. Like any ideological movement, there was fussing and feuding, and Gloria was the one who could get it done. . . . She really worked to raise money for everyone's feminist causes. They'd all come begging to Gloria because she could do it, and they didn't mind exploiting it.* [2]

FEUD WITH FRIEDAN

All Steinem's hard work made her even more visible, and running

Overediting?

At *Ms.*, many editors worked on each article. In addition to polishing the writing, editors also were careful to make sure pieces did not offend anyone based on race, sexual orientation, or economic status. However, the articles went through so many rounds of changes that at times the writers lost their individual voices. Steinem biographer, Sydney Ladensohn Stern explained, "In their desire to be democratic, positive, and inclusive, the editors committed excesses—editing to the point of homogenization, inclusivity to the point of silliness, positivity sometimes to the point of distortion, cliquishness to the point of favoritism, self-promotion to the point of exaggeration (there seemed to be a *Ms.* view of feminist history). Their contributions far outstripped their faults, though, and *Ms.* became the voice for the second wave of feminism."[3]

a magazine meant she had a more powerful
megaphone for her ideas than anyone else in
the movement. Soon other prominent feminists
began to challenge her authority. For some time,
Steinem was more radical than Betty Friedan and
had been at odds with her over the direction of
the women's movement. Friedan wanted to focus
primarily on women's opportunities for meaningful
work outside the home. She did not think that
feminism should be distracted by issues such as
lesbianism or racial equality. Steinem thought that
all of these issues were important and that lesbians
and people of color should have equal standing
in the feminist movement. In 1972, Steinem was
chosen by the National Women's Political Caucus
to be its spokesperson at the Democratic National
Convention—a post that Friedan had wanted. This
slight fueled Friedan's dislike of Steinem.

Later that year, Friedan wrote an editorial in
McCall's and held a press conference in which she
blasted Steinem and her colleagues for being too
divisive. She thought they were alienating men,
as well as women who enjoyed being married and
raising children. The *Ms.* women leaped to Steinem's
defense, but Steinem was more measured in her

*Betty Friedan accused Steinem of alienating
some people from the feminist movement.*

response, saying: "Having been falsely accused
by the male establishment journalists of liking
men too much, I am now falsely accused by a
woman establishment journalist of not liking them
enough."[4] Steinem met with more controversy in
1973, however. In a speech to the League of Women
Voters, she compared the work of housewives to
that of maids and prostitutes. She insisted later

that she was criticizing the institution of traditional marriage, not the women themselves, but the damage had been done.

A Phony Feminist?

A more unexpected attack came from another group of feminists—the Redstockings. While more radical than Friedan, Steinem was moderate compared to radical groups such as the Redstockings, some of whom refused to work within the existing political system or wanted to completely transform society. However, Steinem agreed with many of the radicals' views and considered them to be allies.

In 1967, it had become public that the CIA had funded the Independent Research Service in its efforts to help US citizens attend the youth festivals. At that time, Steinem had gone on national television to explain what the group had been doing and her part in it. She made clear that the CIA had not influenced her or asked her to spy on Americans or foreigners.

But eight years later, the connection came back to haunt her. A group of Redstockings released a 16-page press release titled "Redstockings Discloses Gloria Steinem's CIA Cover-up." It took Steinem's known association with the CIA one step further. They accused her of not being a legitimate feminist, but a CIA plant. The government agency had been known in the past to infiltrate groups working for political change to influence them or to secretly support more moderate groups as alternatives. The women of Redstockings feared that the CIA had a problem with the success of the radical women's movement and had enlisted Steinem to replace it with a weakened version through *Ms.* Furthermore, they thought all

---

Trashing

In a movement so large, there were bound to be women who disagreed with each other over what issues feminism should take on or how extreme the solutions should be. Feminists disagreed about whether the movement should address reproductive choice, lesbianism, and racial issues. Some believed change would come through national groups such as NOW, while others believed in the power of small consciousness-raising sessions. More moderate feminists wanted to work within the current political and societal structures, while radicals wanted to change the system of male domination completely. Instead of intelligent debate, however, these disagreements often led to personal attacks among prominent feminists. The practice became so widespread that it came to be called "trashing." Jo Freeman wrote about the effects of trashing in a 1976 article for *Ms.*:

> Trashing is an incredibly vicious form of character assassination which amounts to psychological rape. It is manipulative, dishonest, and excessive. It is occasionally disguised by the rhetoric of honest conflict. . . . But it is not done to expose disagreements or to resolve differences. It is done to disparage and destroy.[5]

the organizations to which Steinem belonged—such as the Women's Action Alliance—were collecting personal information on individuals to share with the CIA.

Although Friedan's feminist views differed widely from those of the radical Redstockings, she joined them in their criticisms. She publicly talked about Steinem's connections to the CIA and then alluded to them in her book *It Changed My Life*. Among other criticisms in the book, she wrote that Steinem was a master manipulator and that she and other radical feminists drove mainstream Americans away from the women's movement.

It seemed that Steinem could not please anyone. In the view of Friedan and the NOW women, she was too extreme. In the view of radicals such as the Redstockings, she was not extreme enough. Although the media had largely ignored

Long-Term Relationships

Steinem had two significant romantic relationships in the 1970s. From 1971 to 1974, she was involved with Franklin Thomas, who ran a successful urban-renewal project. They met when Steinem was assigned to write about Thomas for *New York*. The two were very close, but Thomas was going through some difficult times. One reason the two parted was because the relationship reminded Steinem of the caretaker relationship she once had with her mother.

In 1974, Steinem met Stan Pottinger of the US Justice Department when he interviewed her for a task force on women's issues. The two hit it off. They stayed together until 1984.

it, the Redstockings' accusation was particularly
painful. Feminism had become her life's purpose,
and for that to be disbelieved hurt her deeply. She
responded with a six-page letter sent to several
feminist publications. Unfortunately, her detailed
explanations drew more attention to the controversy.

Steinem, far left, faced some criticism for her background and methods, but many still considered her a vital part of the women's movement.

Steinem spoke at the Democratic National Convention in 1972.

CELEBRATIONS AND
SETBACKS

Steinem had other problems besides attacks from fellow feminists. Despite its popularity and her efforts, *Ms.* continued to struggle financially. This was in part due to the fact that Steinem and Carbine's feminist principles influenced the magazine's business side. Not only did they charge more for advertising than other women's magazines, but Steinem and Carbine worked hard to attract advertisers who did not traditionally reach out to women. They were also choosy about advertisements, refusing to run any ads that they felt reinforced gender stereotypes. Making the task more difficult, many advertisers did not want to be associated with anything controversial. They preferred to run an ad next to a fashion spread than an article about abortion or domestic violence. Conflicts between Steinem and other feminists worsened the situation by creating bad publicity for *Ms.* The result was that *Ms.* was not able to pay its writers and editors as much as it wished. Its staff continued to contribute out of dedication to the cause. Steinem herself often did not draw her paycheck and donated her speaking fees to *Ms.*

The founders of *Ms.* had originally hoped to donate some of the magazine's earnings back to

Almost Banned

In 1978, a school board in Nashua, New Hampshire, became the first to try to ban copies of *Ms.* from its high school library. A local court intervened to prevent the removal. In 1980, a coalition of 700 parents formed in Contra Costa, California, to pressure the school board into banning *Ms.* In the words of one of its leaders, "*Ms.* would be rated 'X' if it was a movie."[1] Following a 3 to 2 vote along gender lines, a compromise was reached. The school libraries continued to carry *Ms.*, but students had to obtain permission from a parent and a teacher to have access.

the women's movement. In spite of their financial struggles, Steinem and her partners had created the Ms. Foundation for Women in 1972 and conducted fund-raising for it. The foundation helped many women in need— from battered women to female politicians. By the late 1970s, it ended up helping the magazine itself. After much consideration, Steinem and Carbine decided to apply for nonprofit status. Instead of a business enterprise, the magazine would now be a publication of the Ms. Foundation for Women. This

---

The Ms. Foundation for Women

When she started *Ms.* magazine in 1972, Steinem saw a need not only for a feminist publication, but for a foundation benefiting women as well. Ms. Foundation for Women was the first foundation that existed to give money to women's causes across race and class. Its founding board members were Steinem, Carbine, Letty Pogrebin, and Marlo Thomas. The founding board members conducted all of the group's fund-raising until a full-time executive director was hired in 1975. The foundation's leaders decided to focus on programs regarding employment, safety, reproductive rights, and issues related to young girls, such as teen pregnancy. In addition to providing funding assistance, they hoped their involvement would shed light on these issues.

One of the foundation's most well-known fund-raising efforts was the production of the classic children's album *Free to Be . . . You and Me,* featuring music, stories, and poems that promote the themes of tolerance, self-esteem, individualism, and gender equality. Thomas got the idea when she was shopping for a gift for her niece and was disappointed in the sexist themes found in children's books and music. The album was made into a successful television special featuring Michael Jackson in 1974.

change allowed them to pursue grants and saved approximately $600,000 per year. As a nonprofit, they would no longer be able to endorse political candidates, although they could still write about politicians and political issues. This move did not solve all of *Ms.*'s income problems, but it bought some time.

SAYING GOOD-BYE

In 1981, Steinem suffered a personal blow when her mother died. Years before, when Ruth had gone to live with her other daughter, Sue, she had finally received the medical care she needed. Ruth began to function more normally, held a part-time job, and was a loving grandmother to Sue's children. When she died in a nursing home at the age of 82, both her daughters were by her side. Steinem was moved to write an essay, "Ruth's Song (Because She Could Not Sing It)," published in 1983 in her first anthology, *Outrageous Acts and Everyday Rebellions*. It was both a stirring tribute and a reflection on the forces that shaped her mother, as well as herself. She wrote:

> *I still don't understand why so many, many years passed before I saw my mother as a person and before I understood*

that many of the forces in her life are patterns women share. Like a lot of daughters, I suppose I couldn't afford to admit that what had happened to my mother was not all personal or accidental, and therefore could happen to me.[2]

"Ruth's Song" was one of two essays that appeared for the first time in *Outrageous Acts and Everyday Rebellions*.

The Infamous Bubble Bath

While Steinem was promoting *Outrageous Acts and Everyday Rebellions*, she shocked everyone by letting a photographer for *People* take her photo in a bubble bath. The decision seemed to contradict all of Steinem's statements that she did not want the media to focus on her appearance. Steinem explained that the woman had wanted to photograph Steinem doing something she found relaxing—and that happened to be taking a bath. Steinem also said in her defense, "Sometimes people confuse feminists with nuns. . . . There's nothing wrong with bodies or sensuality or sexuality. The question is, who controls that."[3]

The anthology also includes a few of Steinem's previously published articles. The book's first section contains essays about her experience going undercover as a Playboy Bunny, political campaigning, joining the feminist movement, and attending her college reunion. Five profiles of prominent women were reprinted. Other essays covered issues related to feminism, such as "Words and Change," "In Praise of Women's Bodies," and "The Importance of Work." The collection was well reviewed and sold approximately 100,000 copies in hardcover. New American Library paid Steinem $220,000 for the paperback rights.

She used part of the advance to start making plans for her eventual retirement.

HIGHS AND LOWS

In 1982, the *Ms.* staff celebrated surviving its first ten years with a gala for 1,200 people. When Steinem turned 50 in 1984, her friends planned another huge party, this time at the Waldorf-Astoria, a luxury hotel in New York City. The black-tie event was not only a way of saying thank you for all Steinem had done for women, but also a fund-raiser for the Ms. Foundation. Actor Marlo Thomas and her husband, talk-show host Phil Donahue, hosted, and actor and singer Bette Midler provided the entertainment. Approximately 800 guests attended, including civil rights icon Rosa Parks, consumer advocate Ralph Nader, news anchors Tom Brokaw and Diane Sawyer, and many other celebrities.

The *Ms.* staff also planned other fund-raising events to benefit the magazine, including annual breakfasts to honor the *Ms.* Woman of the Year. Facing rising production costs, they raised subscription fees and solicited donations. But the magazine continued to be dangerously close to failing—something Steinem desperately wanted to

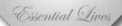
avoid because of how she thought it would reflect on the women's movement.

Steinem had grown exhausted and weary from her efforts to save *Ms.* as well as fulfill all her other obligations. In 20 years, she had traveled every single week but one, and the fast-paced lifestyle had taken its toll. She has blamed her depleted state of mind for leading her into an ill-advised romance with Mort Zuckerman. Zuckerman was a wealthy businessman who disagreed with her politically and was known for his poor treatment of others. Steinem let herself overlook these traits for several years because the romance provided some stress relief. As the couple was finally parting ways, another blow came. In 1986, Steinem found out she had breast cancer. She later said that one of her first thoughts after she was diagnosed was, "I've had a good life."[4] That life was far from over, though.

College Reunion

In 1981, Steinem found out where her fellow Smith classmates had ended up when she attended her twenty-fifth class reunion. A survey of the class showed that 80 percent were married, 5 percent—including Steinem—had never married, and 10 percent had been married twice or more. Less than half were working full-time for pay, while 31 percent were working part-time. But an overwhelming majority—98 percent—identified themselves as pro-choice. In other words, they believed abortion should be legal. Steinem reflected, "Having grown up in the era of illegal abortion, many of us had experienced the danger first-hand."[5]

Steinem continued to enjoy writing and giving speeches into the 1980s.

In 1986, Steinem published a biography of Marilyn Monroe.

STANDING STRONG

he cancer diagnosis did not keep
Steinem down for long. She had the
tumor removed, underwent six weeks of radiation
treatments, and then immediately went on tour for
her latest book, *Marilyn*. It was the first biography of

Marilyn Monroe written by a woman, and Steinem
had written it to fulfill a financial debt that *Ms.* had
to the book's publisher.

Around this time, Steinem also started to
receive another kind of treatment. At the urging of
friends, she began seeing a therapist. Talking with
the therapist helped her work through her mother's
death, the enormous pressures she was facing, and
lingering issues from her childhood.

During this time she continued
her feverish effort to promote *Ms.*,
as well as working on other causes
she believed in. From 1986 to 1987,
for example, she served on the
Citizens' Committee on AIDS for
New York and Upper New Jersey.
The commission created widely used
guidelines for employers on how
to treat employees who have AIDS.
Gay activist Tom Stoddard had high
praise for Steinem's ability to be
both opinionated and respectful
of others on the committee. "She
is a peacemaker, an extraordinary
combination of change-maker and

Honors

In 1993, Steinem was
inducted into the National
Women's Hall of Fame in
Seneca Falls, New York.
She has also received the
Lifetime Achievement in
Journalism Award from
the Society of Professional
Journalists, the Society of
Writers Award from the
United Nations, the Bill
of Rights Award from the
American Civil Liberties
Union, the National Gay
Rights Advocates Award,
and the Liberty Award
of the Lambda Legal
Defense and Education
Fund.

peacemaker. I was stunned to find a celebrity who was genuinely humble and kind."[1]

BEYOND *Ms.*

After years of struggling to become profitable, *Ms.* now found itself in a dire financial situation. Steinem and Carbine went looking for investors; instead they found buyers. In 1987, an Australian company purchased the magazine, with Australian feminist journalist Anne Summers taking over as editor in chief. Trying to entice advertisers and raise circulation, Summers turned *Ms.* into a more general-interest women's magazine that featured celebrities on the cover. But the Australians failed to hold onto *Ms.* for long. It 1989, it was sold again to Lang Communications, publisher of *Working Woman* and *Working Mother*. At this time it became an ad-free and bimonthly publication, solely supported by its subscribers, and returned to its feminist roots. Steinem continued receiving a salary as a consultant. By 1991, the magazine had become profitable, and now that it was ad-free, editors no longer had to worry about offending advertisers.

Free of her overwhelming commitment to *Ms.*, Steinem made some changes in her life, slowing

down ever so slightly. She became an editor at
Random House, picked up two book contracts, and
finally unpacked and furnished her little apartment
in New York City. She threw herself
into writing *Revolution from Within: A
Book of Self-Esteem*, which was published
in 1992. The book, which was
based on her time in therapy, her
research of self-esteem, and her
own life experiences, received mixed
reviews. Some reviewers criticized
it for being a pitiful response to
a midlife crisis or a collection of
useless psychobabble. Others thought
it could potentially be damaging to
feminism because it did not discuss
the societal structures that impact
women's self-esteem. However,
Steinem received an entirely different
response from the women who read it
and used her advice to make changes
in their own lives. Letters of praise
poured in, crowds gathered at book
signings, and the book became a
best seller.

The Fate of *Ms.*

Ms. has changed hands
several more times but
continues to provide in-
depth coverage of issues
related to women. In
1996, Lang sold *Ms.*,
along with *Working
Woman* and *Working
Mother*, to MacDonald
Communications Corp.
The other two magazines
started losing money, and
the staff at all three magazines was downsized.
Steinem and a group of
female investors, under
the name Liberty Media
Women, bought the
magazine back in 1998.
In 2001, the Feminist
Majority Foundation, an
organization that sup-
ports equality for women,
reproductive health, and
nonviolence, acquired
Ms. magazine. As of
2010, the magazine was
still in circulation.

Her next book, *Moving Beyond Words*, was published in 1994. It is a collection of six articles. Three are expanded versions of previous works. The other three are new essays: a witty piece that envisioned famous psychiatrist Sigmund Freud, whose work some viewed as degrading to women, as a woman; a feminist take on economics; and "Doing Sixty," Steinem's reflections on aging.

The Aging Activist

Age has hardly slowed Steinem down. In addition to consulting on *Ms.*, she has served on the advisory board of Feminist.com, an online community and collection of resources regarding women's issues. She has also served on the Board of Trustees for Smith College and cofounded the Women's Media Center in 2005, which promotes women's issues and stories in the media. In her later years, Steinem has continued to remain active and vocal on political issues. She has spoken out against pornography, sexual harassment, and trafficking of women. She has opposed the 2003 war in Iraq. She spoke out against the policies of President George W. Bush, who passed legislation that placed restrictions on abortions and cut funding for family planning services. But she also recognizes the progress that has been made since her early days as a feminist. These days, many women still prioritize marriage and children over ambition and careers. But Steinem recognizes these are individual choices rather than societal pressures.

In 2000, Steinem may have committed one of her most outrageous acts yet. Going against a lifelong principle, she got married. She chose businessman, environmentalist, and animal rights activist David Bale as her spouse. Instead of thinking of themselves as husband and wife, Bale and Steinem called each other "the friend I married."[2] The

"In It for Life"

In *Outrageous Acts and Everyday Rebellions*, Steinem included an essay called "Far From the Opposite Shore," about challenges and strategies in the women's movement. She concluded it by explaining how she had come to devote her lifetime to feminist causes:

In my first days of feminism, I thought I would do this ("this" being feminism) for a few years and then return to my real life (what my "real life" might be, I did not know). Partly, that was a naïve belief that injustice only had to be pointed out in order to be cured. Partly, it was a simple lack of courage.

But like so many others now and in movements past, I've learned that this is not something we care about for a year or two or three. We are in it for life—and for our lives. Not even the spiral of history is needed to show the distance traveled. We have only to look back at the less complete people we ourselves used to be.[3]

couple remained together until Bale
died of a brain lymphoma in 2003.

When questioned about her
decision to finally marry, Steinem
pointed out how much the world
has changed. By 2000, marriage
no longer meant giving up part of
oneself. But that does not mean
feminism has accomplished all it set
out to change. As Steinem told *Time*
magazine after turning 70, young
women may be able to find a job, but
they still are denied promotions. As
long as working women continue to
do the majority of housework and
child rearing, in effect they work two
jobs. More women are in positions of
power, but they are far outnumbered
by men. All these issues—not to
mention reproductive rights, same-
sex marriage, childcare, health care,
racism, poverty, and numerous
others—remain to be addressed.
In Gloria Steinem's eyes, the fight
continues.

Lasting Gift

Steinem has said that
the Ms. Foundation for
Women was as important
to her as the magazine,
and she had hoped to
provide an endowment
to ensure its continued
health. For her sixtieth
birthday, several of her
close friends united to
help make that hap-
pen, raising more than
$2 million in two months.
Friend and prominent
feminist politician Bella
Abzug toasted her at the
party: "We have to think
about what Gloria is and
what she's done. She's
crystallized the emo-
tions and yearnings of
our entire gender. She's
served as our most vivid
expression of our hopes
and demands. She's our
pen and our tongue and
our heart."[4]

As of 2010, Steinem continued to campaign for social causes.

TIMELINE

1934	1956	1956
Gloria Steinem is born on March 25.	Steinem graduates with honors from Smith College.	Steinem earns a scholarship to study in India.

1963	1968	1968
Going undercover as a Playboy Bunny, Steinem writes an exposé about sexism at New York's Playboy Club.	*New York* magazine hires Steinem as a political columnist and features writer.	Steinem supports presidential candidate George McGovern at the Democratic National Convention.

1959	1960	1962
As director of the Independent Research Service, Steinem attends the International Youth Festival in Vienna, Austria.	Upon returning to New York City, Steinem works as a freelance journalist.	Steinem publishes her first major article in *Esquire* magazine.

1968–1969	1969	1969
Steinem publicizes Cesar Chavez's boycott of table grapes.	After attending a Redstockings event, Steinem identifies herself as a feminist.	Steinem writes "After Black Power, Women's Liberation," for *New York* magazine.

TIMELINE

1970	1972	1972
Along with Brenda Feigen, Steinem founds the Women's Action Alliance.	The preview issue of *Ms.* magazine sells out in eight days.	Steinem cofounds the Ms. Foundation for Women.

1992	1993	1994
Little, Brown and Company publishes Steinem's book *Revolution from Within: A Book of Self-Esteem.*	Steinem is inducted into the National Women's Hall of Fame.	Simon & Schuster publishes Steinem's second anthology of essays, *Moving Beyond Words.*

1975	**1983**	**1986**
The Redstockings issue a press release accusing Steinem of working for the CIA rather than being a true feminist.	*Outrageous Acts and Everyday Rebellions*, Steinem's first anthology of essays, is published.	Steinem is diagnosed with breast cancer. Steinem publishes *Marilyn*, a biography of Marilyn Monroe.

1998	**2000**	**2005**
Liberty Media Women, led by Steinem, acquires control of *Ms.* magazine.	Steinem marries David Bale. They remain married until Bale's death in 2003.	Steinem cofounds the Women's Media Center.

Essential Facts

Date of Birth

March 25, 1934

Place of Birth

Toledo, Ohio

Parents

Leo and Ruth (Nuneviller) Steinem

Education

Western High School
Smith College

Marriage

David Bale (2000–2003)

Children

None

Career Highlights

After years struggling to be taken seriously as a freelance journalist, Steinem joined the feminist movement in 1969. She immediately began promoting women's causes through writing and extensive lecturing. Seeing a need for a national publication dedicated to feminist ideas, in 1972 she cofounded *Ms.* magazine. She has also published several successful books, including *Outrageous Acts and Everyday Rebellions*, *Moving Beyond Words*, and *Revolution from Within: A Book of Self-Esteem*.

SOCIETAL CONTRIBUTION

In addition to cofounding, editing, and promoting *Ms.*, Steinem continued her political activism and became one of the most visible and influential leaders of the feminist movement. She has fought for equality in the workplace, reproductive rights, and many other women's rights. Steinem also helped create several feminist organizations, including Women's Action Alliance, Ms. Foundation for Women, and the Women's Media Center.

CONFLICTS

As a leader of the women's movement, Steinem sometimes found herself in disagreement with others about what feminism should encompass. Betty Friedan criticized her for being too extreme and for alienating men, as well as women who had chosen to be wives and mothers. Some radical feminists, on the other hand, thought her approach was too mild. In 1975, a group of radicals called the Redstockings falsely accused her of working for the CIA to foil the women's movement.

QUOTE

"Women who write, like Negroes who write, are supposed to be specialists on themselves, and little else. Newspapers and magazines are generous with assignments on fashion, beauty and childbirth. (Would men like to write about hunting, shaving, and paternity?) But scientific or economic or political stories have a way of gravitating somewhere else." —*Gloria Steinem*

GLOSSARY

abortion
The termination of a pregnancy.

boycott
Refusal to purchase certain goods as a form of protest.

consciousness-raising
An increasing of public awareness about a political or social cause.

conservative
Supportive of traditional ideas and values; tending to resist change to existing views, conditions, or institutions.

contraception
Deliberate prevention of pregnancy.

demonstration
A public display of group feelings toward a person or cause.

domestic violence
The inflicting of physical injury by one family member on another.

endowment
An organization's income from donations.

feminism
Belief in political, social, and economic equality of the sexes; organized activity on behalf of women's rights and social justice.

freelancer
A person who pursues a profession without a longtime commitment to any one employer.

ideals
Ultimate purposes or standards of excellence.

liberation movement
A movement of seeking equal rights and status for a group.

pro-choice
  Favoring the legalization of abortion.

radical
  Supporting big changes in existing views, institutions, and conditions.

sexism
  Prejudice or discrimination based on sex.

sexual harassment
  Uninvited, unwelcome behavior of a sexual nature, especially by a person of authority.

speak-out
  An event at which people publicly share their views or experiences on an issue.

sterilization
  Intentional ending of the ability to reproduce, usually through medical means.

suffrage
  The right to vote.

ADDITIONAL RESOURCES

SELECTED BIBLIOGRAPHY

Heilbrun, Carolyn. *The Education of a Woman: The Life of Gloria Steinem*. New York: The Dial, 1995. Print.

Steinem, Gloria. *Moving Beyond Words*. New York: Simon and Schuster, 1994. Print.

Steinem, Gloria. *Outrageous Acts and Everyday Rebellions*. New York: Holt, Rinehart and Winston, 1983. Print.

Stern, Sydney Ladensohn. *Gloria Steinem: Her Passion, Politics, and Mystique*. Secaucus, NJ: Carol, 1997. Print.

Thom, Mary. *Inside Ms.: 25 Years of the Magazine and the Feminist Movement*. New York: Henry Holt, 1997. Print.

FURTHER READINGS

Gorman, Jacqueline Laks. *Gloria Steinem*. Milwaukee, WI: World Almanac Library, 2004. Print.

Schomp, Virginia. *The Women's Movement*. New York: Marshall Cavendish Benchmark, 2007. Print.

Treanor, Nick. *The Feminist Movement*. San Diego, CA: Greenhaven Press, 2002. Print.

Web Links

To learn more about Gloria Steinem, visit ABDO Publishing
Company online at **www.abdopublishing.com**. Web sites about
Gloria Steinem are featured on our Book Links page. These links
are routinely monitored and updated to provide the most current
information available.

Places to Visit

The National Women's Hall of Fame
76 Fall Street, Seneca Falls, NY 13148
315-568-8060
http://www.greatwomen.org
The National Women's Hall of Fame houses many artifacts relating
to women's movements and women's achievements throughout
US history.

The Women's Museum
3800 Parry Avenue, Dallas, TX 75226
214-915-0860
http://www.thewomensmuseum.org
The Women's Museum focuses on women's past and current
accomplishments and experiences.

Source Notes

Chapter 1. Breaking Free

1. Sydney Ladensohn Stern. *Gloria Steinem: Her Passion, Politics, and Mystique*. Secaucus, NJ: Carol, 1997. Print. 70.

2. Gloria Steinem. *Outrageous Acts and Everyday Rebellions*. New York: Holt, Rinehart and Winston, 1983. Print. 120.

3. Sydney Ladensohn Stern. *Gloria Steinem: Her Passion, Politics, and Mystique*. Secaucus, NJ: Carol, 1997. Print. Ibid. 85.

Chapter 2. Childhood

1. Sydney Ladensohn Stern. *Gloria Steinem: Her Passion, Politics, and Mystique*. Secaucus, NJ: Carol, 1997. Print. 27.

2. Ibid.

3. Carolyn Heilbrun. *The Education of a Woman: The Life of Gloria Steinem*. New York: The Dial, 1995. Print. 24.

4. Carolyn Heilbrun. *The Education of a Woman: The Life of Gloria Steinem*. New York: The Dial, 1995. Print. 20.

5. Ibid. 9.

6. Ibid. 61.

7. Ibid. 59.

Chapter 3. International Adventures

1. Carolyn Heilbrun. *The Education of a Woman: The Life of Gloria Steinem*. New York: The Dial, 1995. Print. 75.

2. Ibid. 74.

3. Ibid. 81–82.

4. Ibid. 76.

5. Sydney Ladensohn Stern. *Gloria Steinem: Her Passion, Politics, and Mystique*. Secaucus, NJ: Carol, 1997. Print. 118.

Chapter 4. An Aspiring Writer

1. Sydney Ladensohn Stern. *Gloria Steinem: Her Passion, Politics, and Mystique*. Secaucus, NJ: Carol, 1997. Print. 126.

2. Margalit Fox. "Betty Friedan, Who Ignited Cause in 'Feminine Mystique,' Dies at 85." *New York Times*. The New York Times Company, 5 Feb. 2006. Web. 6 Jun. 2010.

3. Sydney Ladensohn Stern. *Gloria Steinem: Her Passion, Politics, and Mystique*. Secaucus, NJ: Carol, 1997. Print. 137.

4. Ibid. 130.

5. Gloria Steinem. *Outrageous Acts and Everyday Rebellions*. New York: Holt, Rinehart and Winston, 1983. Print. 53.

6. Carolyn Heilbrun. *The Education of a Woman: The Life of Gloria Steinem*. New York: The Dial, 1995. Print. 107.

7. Sydney Ladensohn Stern. *Gloria Steinem: Her Passion, Politics, and Mystique*. Secaucus, NJ: Carol, 1997. Print. 139.

Chapter 5. Political Activism

1. Carolyn Heilbrun. *The Education of a Woman: The Life of Gloria Steinem*. New York: The Dial, 1995. Print. 145.

2. Ibid. 144.

3. Gloria Steinem. "Herstory: Finding the Enormous Gift." *Mother Jones*. Nov. 1977. Print. 69.

4. Carolyn Heilbrun. *The Education of a Woman: The Life of Gloria Steinem*. New York: The Dial, 1995. Print. 126.

Source Notes Continued

Chapter 6. Finding Feminism
1. Carolyn Heilbrun. *The Education of a Woman: The Life of Gloria Steinem*. New York: The Dial, 1995. Print. 169.
2. Gloria Steinem. *Outrageous Acts and Everyday Rebellions*. New York: Holt, Rinehart and Winston, 1983. Print. 17.
3. Carolyn Heilbrun. *The Education of a Woman: The Life of Gloria Steinem*. New York: The Dial, 1995. Print. 185.
4. Sydney Ladensohn Stern. *Gloria Steinem: Her Passion, Politics, and Mystique*. Secaucus, NJ: Carol, 1997. Print. 202.
5. Gloria Steinem. *Outrageous Acts and Everyday Rebellions*. New York: Holt, Rinehart and Winston, 1983. Print. 19.
6. Ibid. 149.
7. Carolyn Heilbrun. *The Education of a Woman: The Life of Gloria Steinem*. New York: The Dial, 1995. Print. 192.

Chapter 7. A New Kind of Women's Magazine
1. Mary Thom. *Inside Ms.: 25 Years of the Magazine and the Feminist Movement*. New York: Henry Holt, 1997. Print. 14.
2. Ibid. 25.
3. Ibid. 20.

Chapter 8. An Embattled Leader
1. Mary Thom. *Inside Ms.: 25 Years of the Magazine and the Feminist Movement*. New York: Henry Holt, 1997. Print. 54.
2. Sydney Ladensohn Stern. *Gloria Steinem: Her Passion, Politics, and Mystique*. Secaucus, NJ: Carol, 1997. Print. 284–285.
3. Ibid. 276.
4. Mary Thom. *Inside Ms.: 25 Years of the Magazine and the Feminist Movement*. New York: Henry Holt, 1997. Print. 51.
5. Jo Freeman. "Trashing: the Dark Side of Sisterhood." *JoFreeman.com*. n.p., Apr. 1976. Web. 6 Jun. 2010.

Chapter 9. Celebrations and Setbacks

1. Sydney Ladensohn Stern. *Gloria Steinem: Her Passion, Politics, and Mystique*. Secaucus, NJ: Carol, 1997. Print. 286.

2. Gloria Steinem. *Outrageous Acts and Everyday Rebellions*. New York: Holt, Rinehart and Winston, 1983. Print. 144.

3. Sydney Ladensohn Stern. *Gloria Steinem: Her Passion, Politics, and Mystique*. Secaucus, NJ: Carol, 1997. Print. 340.

4. Ibid. 365.

5. Gloria Steinem. *Revolution from Within: A Book of Self-Esteem*. Boston: Little, Brown, 1992. Print. 113.

Chapter 10. Standing Strong

1. Carolyn Heilbrun. *The Education of a Woman: The Life of Gloria Steinem*. New York: The Dial, 1995. Print. 386.

2. Melissa Denes. "Feminism? It's hardly begun." *guardian.co.uk*. Guardian News and Media Limited, 17 Jan. 2005. Web. 6 Jun. 2010.

3. Gloria Steinem. *Outrageous Acts and Everyday Rebellions*. New York: Holt, Rinehart and Winston, 1983. Print. 361–362.

4. Sydney Ladensohn Stern. *Gloria Steinem: Her Passion, Politics, and Mystique*. Secaucus, NJ: Carol, 1997. Print. 439.

INDEX

ABOUT THE AUTHOR

Erika Wittekind is a freelance writer and editor living in Wisconsin. She has a bachelor of arts degree in journalism and political science from Bradley University. Wittekind has covered education and government for several community newspapers, winning an award for best local news story from the Minnesota Newspapers Association in 2002.

PHOTO CREDITS

Todd Plitt/Getty Images, cover, 3; AP Images, 6, 39, 44, 74, 80, 96 (bottom); Werner Rings/Getty Images, 11; Yale Joel/Time & Life Pictures/Getty Images, 13, 52; Ron Galella/WireImage/Getty Images, 14; Peter Stackpole/Time & Life Pictures/Getty Images, 23, 96 (top); George Marks/Getty Images, 24; James A. Mills/AP Images, 26; Susan Wood/Getty Images, 33; Jennifer Graylock/AP Images, 34; Hulton Archive/Getty Images, 43, 97; Blank Archives/Getty Images, 46; Bob Wands/AP Images, 51; Jim Wells/AP Images, 58, 61; Dave Pickoff/AP Images, 62, 98; New York Daily News Archive/NY Daily News/Getty Images, 69; CBS Photo Archive/CBS/Getty Images, 70; Michael Abramson/Time & Life Pictures/Getty Images, 79; Ted Powers/AP Images, 87; Gill Allen/AP Images, 88, 99 (top); Judi Bottoni/AP Images, 95, 99 (bottom)